The HARLEM RENAISSANCE

HEDREICH NICHOLS WITH KELISA WING

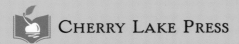
CHERRY LAKE PRESS

Published in the United States of America by Cherry Lake Publishing Group
Ann Arbor, Michigan
www.cherrylakepublishing.com

Reading Adviser: Beth Walker Gambro, MS, Ed., Reading Consultant, Yorkville, IL
Content Adviser: Kelisa Wing
Book Design and Cover Art: Felicia Macheske

Photo Credits: © travelwild/Shutterstock.com, 5; U.S. National Archives, The Harmon Foundation, Identifier: 559227, 6; © classicpaintings/Alamy Stock Photo, 6; © Science History Images/Alamy Stock Photo, 9; Library of Congress, Photo by Alan Fisher, LOC Control No: 99403374, 11; © Sueddeutsche Zeitung Photo/Alamy Stock Photo, 12; Library of Congress, William P. Gottlieb Collection, 15; © dpa picture alliance/Alamy Stock Photo, 16; U.S. National Archives, The Harmon Foundation, Identifier: 26174894, 19; New York Public Library: *digitalcollections.nypl.org/items/898ec0bf-39fb-92e7-e040-e00a18063ff1*, 21; U.S. National Archives, The Harmon Foundation, Identifier: 559078, 23; New York Public Library: *digitalcollections.nypl.org/items/6ca557ed-9597-5dcd-e040-e00a18065af4*, 24; © Gavin Hellier/Alamy Stock Photo, 27; © chomplearn/Shutterstock.com, 29

Graphics Throughout: © debra hughes/Shutterstock.com; © Galyna_P/Shutterstock.com

Library of Congress Cataloging-in-Publication Data

Names: Nichols, Hedreich, author. | Wing, Kelisa, author.
Title: The Harlem Renaissance / by Hedreich Nichols and Kelisa Wing.
Description: Ann Arbor, Michigan : Cherry Lake Publishing, [2022] |
    Series: Racial justice : excellence and achievement | Audience: Grades 7-9 |
    Summary: "The music, literature, and culture that came out of the Harlem Renaissance is still celebrated today—and continues to influence art around the world. This book explores the people and places that made the era so important. The Racial Justice in America: Excellence and Achievement series celebrates Black achievement and culture, while exploring racism in a comprehensive, honest, and age-appropriate way. Developed in conjunction with educator, advocate, and author Kelisa Wing to reach children of all races and encourage them to approach our history with open eyes and minds. Books include 21st Century Skills and content, activities created by Wing, table of contents, glossary, index, author biography, sidebars, and educational matter"—Provided by publisher.
Identifiers: LCCN 2021047059 | ISBN 9781534199309 (hardcover) | ISBN 9781668900444 (paperback) | ISBN 9781668906200 (ebook) | ISBN 9781668901885 (pdf)
Subjects: LCSH: African American arts—New York (State)—New York—20th century—Juvenile literature. | Harlem Renaissance—Juvenile literature.
Classification: LCC NX512.3.A35 N54 2022 | DDC 700.89/9607307471—dc23/eng/20211018
LC record available at https://lccn.loc.gov/2021047059

Cherry Lake Publishing Group would like to acknowledge the work of the Partnership for 21st Century Learning, a Network of Battelle for Kids. Please visit *http://www.battelleforkids.org/networks/p21* for more information.

Printed in the United States of America
Corporate Graphics

Hedreich Nichols, author, educator, and host of the YouTube series on equity #SmallBites, is a retired Grammy-nominated singer-songwriter turned EdTech teacher who uses her experience as a "one Black friend" to help others understand race, equity, and how to celebrate diversity. When not educating and advocating, she enjoys making music with her son, multi-instrumentalist @SwissChrisOnBass.

Kelisa Wing honorably served in the U.S. Army and has been an educator for 14 years. She is the author of *Promises and Possibilities: Dismantling the School to Prison Pipeline*, *If I Could: Lessons for Navigating an Unjust World*, and *Weeds & Seeds: How to Stay Positive in the Midst of Life's Storms*. She speaks both nationally and internationally about discipline reform, equity, and student engagement. Kelisa lives in Northern Virginia with her husband and two children.

CHAPTER 1

What Was the Harlem Renaissance?

The word *renaissance* is a word that means a rebirth or awakening, especially of culture, art, science, and philosophy. In the early 1900s, the Harlem area of New York City became the center of such a movement. This renaissance in the Black community and the appreciation for Black art, philosophy, and culture impacted not only people in Harlem but also those in communities around the world. The Harlem Renaissance lasted until the mid-1930s, but its effects are still felt today.

Harlem is a bustling area of New York City north of Central Park.

Lois Mailou Jones
and her work.

Because the North offered Black families a better life, hundreds of thousands of African Americans moved from the South to the North in the early 1900s. This was the first wave of what was called the Great Migration. Harlem in Manhattan, New York, was one of the places that attracted Black people to start a new life. Life in New York was different because New York did not have the oppressive Jim Crow laws of the South.

The Harlem Renaissance was a time of great racial pride when other cultures began to recognize and appreciate Black music, dance, literature, and art. It was an important and uplifting phase for Black people, even those who didn't live in Harlem.

Many Black artists moved to Europe where they did not have to face segregation and discrimination. Artists like Lois Mailou Jones and writers like James Baldwin moved to Paris, France. They found that racism was not a big factor in a foreign country. They were two notable Harlem Renaissance influencers who found more freedom outside the United States than in it.

CHAPTER 2

Music & Dance

One of the most well-known developments of the Harlem Renaissance came from the musical community. Beginning with Scott Joplin's ragtime music in the early 1900s, jazz and blues expanded on the new rhythm patterns found in music like "The Entertainer" to develop swing. Swing was what made jazz and blues different and more lively—kind of like the difference between marching band music and hip-hop. Jazz and blues were also more exciting because they were improvisational. This means that singers or musicians make up the melody on the spot, like making a speech without written notes. Jazz and blues influenced other modern types of music like pop, rock, hip-hop, and gospel.

Boxing champion, Jack Johnson, opened the Cotton Club (originally
called The Club Deluxe) in 1920.

Many famous artists of the day performed at Harlem night spots like the Lenox, the Cotton Club, the Savoy Ballroom, the Apollo Theater, and others. Performers like blues singer Bessie Smith, drummer and bandleader Chick Webb, singer and dancer Adelaide Hall, and pianist James Price Johnson were pioneers and leaders in the entertainment industry. Similarly, jazz orchestra or "big band" leaders such as Duke Ellington, Fletcher Henderson, and Count Basie proved to be some of the most influential composers of all time. You can watch videos of them perform on YouTube today.

Before the recording industry was integrated, companies recognized the potential of diverse music styles. They created "Race Music" divisions to find, produce, and promote Black artists to Black listeners. While this new market allowed artists to be heard across America, the companies used the Black artists' lack of business knowledge to their advantage. They paid artists little or nothing. Many artists also lost the rights to their music. That meant many popular artists of that era were well known but still lived in poverty.

Jazz in Church— Sort of

The influence of jazz music was also felt in the Black church, although churches hesitated at first to mix what they sometimes referred to as "devil's music" with hymns and spirituals. Still, Pastor Adam Clayton Powell Jr. recognized the importance of this new sound by supporting a talented young musician. According to reputable reports, Powell would sneak Thomas "Fats" Waller into his father's church at night to practice on the big church organ. Of course, this was long before Powell took over the pastoring job from his father. At 15, Fats Waller was already a recognized professional, playing live music at the local theater to accompany silent movies. He later became one of the best-known Black American musicians to compose, play multiple instruments, and record for national recording companies.

Thomas "Fats" Waller

The dance called the "Charleston" started in Black communities, but soon people all over the country were learning the moves.

With the new "ragged time" rhythms of jazz and blues came new ways of moving to music. Popular dances like the Lindy Hop, Shimmy, Charleston, Shuffle Along, and Cakewalk began in the Black community. These dances were characterized by movements that were livelier than the popular dances of that time. People who danced the new dances also improvised. They began with a pattern but added their own movements as they went along. In the Lindy Hop, for example, tumbling and gymnastic elements were used. In the Shimmy, dancers used fast shoulder shaking based on the Nigerian Shika dance.

Even though there was no TikTok, these dance trends spread when people traveled to Harlem to dance and then took the dances back to their own communities. Unlike today's short-lived viral trends, dances like the Charleston are still talked about today. Partner swing dances that evolved from the Lindy Hop are still being danced around the world. As a matter of fact, near the end of both *Fortnite*'s Shake It Up emote and the TikTok *Whole Shack Shimmy Challenge* is a 1900s Shimmy!

Some of the best-known writers, composers, dancers, and singers combined their talents in musicals, which are theater productions with singing and dancing. Up until the Harlem Renaissance period, most "Black" theater consisted of minstrel shows.

Unlike minstrel shows, the theater productions and musicals of the Harlem Renaissance period portrayed real-life Black people instead of stereotypes. Productions like *In Dahomey* and *Shuffle Along* were written for and performed by Black people. *Shuffle Along* was a lively musical that was the first all-Black Broadway production. The cast of *Shuffle Along* gave 504 performances, making it a huge Broadway hit in its time.

Scat Master

Cab Calloway was a famous bandleader, singer, and dancer who was a regular performer at Harlem's Cotton Club. Calloway was famous for using "scat" in his music. Scat was a type of vocal improvisation that used syllables with no meaning instead of words. During his career, which lasted almost 70 years, he performed live, appeared in at least 26 movies, and recorded many albums as a bandleader or singer. Calloway had 45 top-100 songs, most of which landed in the top 20. Even by modern chart standards, this was an extraordinary achievement. He was named to the **Grammy** Hall of Fame.

Cab Calloway

Langston Hughes was famous for his mastery of jazz poetry, an art form that combines the rhythm of jazz with the words of poetry.

Not all theater productions were lighthearted. A more serious play written by the prominent Harlem Renaissance writer Langston Hughes was called *Mulatto*. It was about the conflicts between the children of enslaved mothers and slave-owner fathers who did not acknowledge their children. Although it was a heavy subject, it was a popular play, running on Broadway for almost a year in the 1930s.

The stars of the minstrel shows were not Black people. Instead, the actors were White people in crude Black makeup known as "blackface." These shows made fun of Black people in mean ways and were popular after the Civil War. The stereotypes minstrel shows used became popular too. They were racist, portraying Black characters as simple-minded, lazy, and poor. One of the first popular blackface characters was Jim Crow. The harsh laws designed to oppress Black communities were named for this character.

CHAPTER 3

Literature & Art

Just as the music and dance of the Harlem Renaissance has influenced culture worldwide throughout the last 100 years, the influence of writers, philosophers, and intellectuals from the Harlem Renaissance can still be felt today.

Alain Locke was a Harvard graduate, a Rhodes Scholar, and a professor at historically Black Howard University. He was called the dean of the Harlem Renaissance movement. Even though he didn't live in Harlem, he published a paper about Harlem being the home and birthplace of the "New Negro." That paper became a book and then a movement.

Locke is credited with giving a name to the cultural revolution that spurred the Harlem Renaissance.

The New Negro, according to Locke and other renaissance philosophers, were people of African descent who rejected the stereotypes of the day. They viewed themselves as self-reliant, capable, and worthy of equitable treatment. Considering the social and economic struggles the first generations of freedmen faced, some people considered their views very forward thinking. But Locke was also realistic, acknowledging not only the value and potential of the New Negro, but also the struggle. Locke encouraged others to write, sing, and create art about the experiences of Black people, both the beautiful and the painful ones.

Zora Neale Hurston was one person who portrayed authentic Black life in her writing. She wrote four novels, two books of African American folk tales, and many articles, plays, short stories, and essays. Hurston's most famous book, *Their Eyes Were Watching God*, is a story of an independent woman, which was a rare theme in that day. It uses the Southern dialect of the time to explore the complexities of race and relationships. Although the book received negative criticism when it was written, it's one of the most enduring works from the Harlem Renaissance period.

Hurston's novel, *Their Eyes Were Watching God*, was made into an award-winning movie in 2005.

Locke and Hurston were only two of the many artists and thinkers who influenced the Harlem Renaissance. The works of authors W. E. B. Du Bois, Langston Hughes, Jessie Redmon Fauset, and James Weldon Johnson also influenced that period and the New Negro. Writers of the Harlem Renaissance created work that continues to influence writers, philosophers, and artists throughout the world.

As with music, dance, and literature, the Harlem Renaissance visual artists featured the beauty and intelligence of Black Americans in their work. One such artist was Sargent Johnson. He worked as a painter, potter, carver, and sculptor and was famous throughout the country. His art, which was also influenced by Native American and Mexican art, was respected by the artists in Harlem, and he was counted among them.

"It is the pure American Negro I am concerned with, aiming to show the natural beauty and dignity in that characteristic lip and that characteristic hair, bearing, and manner..."

—Sargent Johnson, Harlem Renaissance artist

Finding Success Too Late

The term "starving artist" describes an artist who can't make enough money to live comfortably. Art often isn't appreciated when it is created. Many visual artists would be millionaires or billionaires if they could only live 50 to 100 years longer. Sargent Johnson was no different. In fact, in 2009, about 50 years after his death, some of his carved wooden artwork was discovered in a storage area at the University of California, Berkeley. It was sold to a local art and furniture dealer for $165. When it was identified, it was found to be worth more than $1 million!

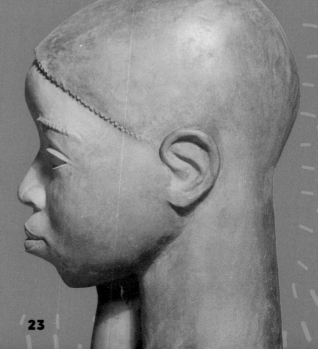

"Chester" 1931: portrait of an African American boy, by Sargent Johnson

Another well-known artist was Aaron Douglas. His artwork is featured in Alain Locke's work, *The New Negro*. He was a painter, illustrator, and muralist who is considered the "father" of Harlem Renaissance artwork. One of his most famous murals, *Aspects of Negro Life*, was painted for the 135th Branch of the New York Public Library in Harlem. It is part of the New York Public Library collections today.

Aspects of Negro Life: Song of the Towers by Aaron Douglas

The Harlem Renaissance produced many painters, sculptors, illustrators, potters, and artists of every kind. There were women artists like painter Lois Mailou Jones and sculptor Augusta Savage. Lois Mailou Jones became famous, but she had to secretly enter her artwork in competitions under the names of her White friends. Augusta Savage, who became the first African American member of the National Association of Women Painters and Sculptors, worked in Harlem as an art teacher.

Other artists included photographer James Van Der Zee, whose pictures documented daily life in Harlem, and painter Jacob Lawrence, who was one of the rare artists who was well known and able to support himself before his death in 2000. The work of these artists and many others like them can be viewed on the National Gallery of Art and the Smithsonian American Art Museum websites.

CHAPTER 4

Activism

The writers, singers, dancers, artists, and supporters of the Harlem Renaissance were all activists. Some fought for civil rights by speaking against or writing about discrimination, such as W. E. B. Du Bois, who was the first Black person to receive a PhD from Harvard University.

Some spoke through their art and music like Aaron Douglas and famed jazz singer Billie Holiday.

Some did not consider themselves activists and allowed their art to speak for itself.

Detailed colorful wall mural in Harlem

The Harlem Renaissance began less than 50 years after the end of enslavement. Millions of Black people were learning to live as free Americans in a society that didn't always give them the full rights of American citizens. Many legal and economic barriers to Black success existed. The drivers of the Harlem Renaissance wrote, created, and designed with these barriers in mind. Their books, thoughts, and songs helped the Black community build confidence and self-esteem, even though they faced rejection and oppression from political systems and people outside their communities.

However, the philosophers, writers, musicians, singers, dancers, and artists communicated to the world that their activism was a part of who they were. It was a part of the work they shared with the world.

By sharing their message, they let people know that the African American was more than a freed slave or a citizen struggling for equality. The Harlem Renaissance showed the New Negro—the intellectual, musical, artistic African American—to the world.

Art can express your views, beliefs, and personality. What would your art say to the world?

Making a Way Out of NO WAY!!!

Journaling Your Way to Justice!

Have you ever heard of a vision board? People create vision boards to set goals for their future. You can do the same thing by creating a Justice Journal! In your Justice Journal, you can write your way to a better future for everyone.

Start by taking a notebook and adding things to the cover that represent the kind of world you want to see. You can use magazine clippings, crayons, markers, colored pencils, or words. Just be creative in designing your Justice Journal. It's a place where you will write about the world you want to see and then make a plan to create it!

As we have learned in this book, Black people contributed to the arts. During the Harlem Renaissance, they showed a new way to see Black people as artists, musicians, and authors. They broke barriers, created new sounds, and contributed to American arts and culture. They followed their passion and dreams to create great music, art, and literature.

How do you wish the world viewed you? Who are you? How do you want to share with others your dreams and hopes?

Write or draw in your Justice Journal and share the story of who you are using this prompt:

I AM POEM

I am (two special characteristics you have)

I wonder (something you are actually curious about)

I hear (an imaginary or actual sound)

I see (an imaginary or actual sight)

I want (a desire)

I am (the first line of the poem is repeated)

I pretend (something you actually pretend to do)

I feel (something imaginary)

I touch (an imaginary touch)

I worry (something that really worries you)

I cry (something that makes you sad)

I am (the first line of the poem is repeated)

I understand (something you know to be true)

I say (something you believe in)

I dream (something you actually dream about)

I try (something you make an effort to do)

I hope (something you hope for)

I am (the first line of the poem repeated)

EXTEND YOUR LEARNING

Read about nine people who were central in the cultural awakening of the Harlem Renaissance.
www.biography.com/news/harlem-renaissance-figures

Learn even more about the writers, actors, musicians, and other prominent figures in the Harlem Renaissance.
artsedge.kennedy-center.org/interactives/harlem/faces/index.html

Watch classic vintage clips of people doing dances from and inspired by the Harlem Renaissance.
www.youtube.com/playlist?list=PLXuPJeS8W-KowM86TF-DauuN3xH_xBQcT

View the artwork of Sargent Johnson and hear him speak in this San Francisco Museum of Modern Art online exhibit.
www.sfmoma.org/artist/sargent_johnson/

View Aaron Douglas's mural, *Aspects of Negro Life*, here. View other collections on the site to see other prominent diverse artists and artwork.
digitalcollections.nypl.org/items/634ad849-7832-309e-e040-e00a180639bb

GLOSSARY

Broadway (BROHD-way) the world-famous theater district of New York City

dean (DEEN) the head of a university or university department

divisions (duh-VIH-shuhnz) departments or subsidiaries of a company

equitable (EH-kwuh-tuh-buhl) dealing fairly and equally with everyone

freedmen (FREED-mahn) people freed from enslavement

Grammy (GRAH-mee) an award from the recording industry that recognizes musical achievement

Jim Crow laws (JIM KROH LAWZ) a series of laws common between 1865 and 1965 that kept freed Black people from full rights of U.S. citizenship; also known as Black Codes

Negro (NEE-groh) the polite term for Black people before the terms *Black* and *African American* were used

philosophy (fuh-LAH-suh-fee) the study of thought, logic, and ideas about right and wrong

ragtime (RAG-tyme) an important precursor to jazz music

Rhodes Scholar (ROHDS SKAH-luhr) a prestigious scholarship to attend the University of Oxford in England

stereotypes (STEHR-ee-uh-typz) widely held but fixed and oversimplified images or ideas of a particular type of person or thing

swing (SWING) a style of jazz music